THUMBS UP!

STAYING POSITIVE WITH PARKINSON'S DISEASE

KEVIN M PEYTON

ISBN: 146377947X
ISBN-13: 9781463779474

Thanks to my wife, Annie, and my two sons, Conor and Ryan, for sticking with me and for giving me reason to keep on pushing forward. Thanks to all my friends and family for your support. I was shocked by the community support my family received after my Deep Brain Stimulation surgery. Thank you all as well.

Thanks to my good friend Valentino Joseph Tocci for his help in reviewing this book and for taking the time to provide such tremendous feedback. I could not have completed this book without it.

Finally, thanks to Dr. Baltuch, Dr. Jaggi, Dr. Stern and the entire medical and rehab staff at the "Parkinson's Disease and Movement Disorders Center" in Philadelphia and the medical staff that was involved in my surgery and recovery at Pennsylvania Hospital. You are all superb!

TABLE OF CONTENTS

INTRODUCTION

When I started to conceptualize this book, I was going to just string together some funny stories that happened to me where Parkinson's disease (PD) was involved. Somewhere along the way, I changed my mind and decided to share my overall experience with PD.

As it turned out, I wrote this book for multiple reasons. First of all, I thought it may be helpful to other people with PD, especially those with early onset PD. I thought that many people may find it easier to relate to someone with PD like me. I am just an average guy doing his best to stay positive, despite dealing with this progressively disabling disease, and looking at an uncertain future.

I also wanted to tell my story. There are a couple passages in this book where you might say to yourself, "What does this have to do with PD?" These parts may not directly relate to PD, but they do relate to me, and how I work my way through life with this disease.

It can be difficult to remain upbeat, especially when you know all the symptoms that may occur. There is no guarantee that you will or will not get certain symptoms, so I have decided to take one day at a time, remain active and not dwell on what my life will be in ten or twenty years. I do not know what symptoms I will have, so I try not to spend too much time worrying about it. I meet with my neurologist, Dr. Stern, twice a year to discuss how I am doing overall, and if there are any changes in my symptoms. He also gives me a standard PD exam, where he checks my balance, coordination, and my gait. If new symptoms have arisen, then we deal with them. If there is nothing new, that is even better. If there is a cure in ten years, I would obviously be ecstatic, but I do not count on that. When I was diagnosed in

4

1992, many people thought that there would be a cure in ten years. Obviously, it has not been found yet.

Undoubtedly, you try to plan financially etc., because just like everyone else, you have no choice, and PD adds complexity to that planning. The future is so uncertain and is different for each patient. I have to be prudent, yet I still try not to dwell on negatives that may never happen.

It is amazing how the loss of dopamine in the brain can wreak such havoc on the body of someone with PD ("parkie"). The physical symptoms of the disease can include the following:

- Tremor or shaking, of the hand, arm, or leg when the person is awake and sitting or standing still (resting tremor) that subsides when the person moves the affected body part.
- Stiff muscles (rigidity) and aching muscles. A reduced arm swing on one side when the person is walking that is caused by rigid muscles. Rigidity can

affect the muscles of the legs, face, neck, or other parts of the body, and may cause muscles to feel tired and achy.

- Bradykinesia - slow, limited movement, especially when the person tries to move from a resting position. For instance, it may be difficult to get out of a chair or turn over in bed.
- Weakness of face and throat muscles. Talking and swallowing may become more difficult, and the person may choke, cough, or drool. Speech becomes softer and monotonous. Loss of movement in the facial muscles can cause a fixed, vacant facial expression, often called the "Parkinson's mask."
- Difficulty with walking (gait disturbance) and balance (postural instability). A person with PD is likely to take small steps and shuffle with his or her feet close together, bend forward slightly at the waist (stooped posture), and have trouble turning around. Balance and posture problems may

result in frequent falls. However, these problems usually do not develop until later in the course of the disease.

- Dystonia – painful cramping or curling of the toes or fingers.

I was batting a thousand on the symptoms above prior to the Deep Brain Stimulation (DBS) procedure. My left side was affected by the tremors more than the right, but the right side did tremor periodically. My muscles would ache and feel tight. Massage and stretching have definitely helped with this. Bradykinesia was beginning to take effect. My gait was getting worse to the point where I often shuffled my feet. I was also starting to hunch over a little, which comes with the shuffling feet, because you tend to look down more to avoid tripping. I struggled with talking and swallowing and still do, although they are not as bad as they were. Drooling has a tendency to occur and has not improved. It seems to happen at inopportune times. For instance, one Sunday Mass in front of hundreds of people I was out cold during the sermon, and I was drooling to boot. My oldest son, Conor, had to throw an elbow into my ribs to awaken me. The dystonia was a daily occurrence in my feet. The toes just cramped and curled right under my feet. So, other than the fact that PD makes it difficult to talk, eat, and move, PD never bothered me at all!

Usually, people think that PD only affects the body and movement. What many do not realize is that there are mental and non-motor effects as well, and many times these are more debilitating than the movement and motor effects.

These are some of the mental and non-motor symptoms:

- Cognitive symptoms - The Parkinson's Disease Foundation states that if you have PD, you may experience feelings of anxiety, dementia, or confusion, and a tendency to participate in compulsive behaviors such as gambling. You may also be diagnosed with clinical depression. Depression may be present with additional symptoms such as a loss of appetite, trouble sleeping, unusual fatigue, feeling guilty, being overly self critical, and having a sense of worthlessness.

- Fatigue and changes in memory - You may also notice that you feel excessively tired and have a lack of energy and drive. According to the Michael J Fox Parkinson's Foundation, you may have difficulty initiating or following through with tasks, problems with short-term and long-term memory, which can be mild or severe, and trouble trying to do more than one task at a time. For example, it may be challenging to walk and carry on a conversation at the same time. I can, however, walk and chew gum at the same time! You may also find it harder to recall words during a conversation, and you may process information more slowly than you could before your diagnosis.
- Additional non-motor symptoms - PD may also cause an all over body ache,

unexplained general muscle pain, and cramping. Additional symptoms can include a loss of smell, speech problems, and a drop in blood pressure when you stand up. The New York Presbyterian Hospital claims that symptoms such as difficulty chewing, urinary problems, constipation and skin problems may also be present.

Of the mental/non-motor symptoms, I have trouble thinking things through. I get fatigued easily, and my short term memory is atrocious. I won't even get into the medication side effects. There are too many medications to cover, and different people are impacted in different ways. To me the toughest thing to face for everyone involved would have to be dementia. This is my greatest fear. I have relatives that suffered a great deal from Alzheimer's disease. It puts a tremendous strain on the entire family.

I am forty-five years old now and I was diagnosed when I was twenty-six, so I am working on nineteen years in my relationship with this disease. It really is a relationship in the sense that life with this disease changes day to day, and it throws a monkey wrench in my plans quite often. That line, "Life is like a box of chocolates. You never know what you're gonna' get," from the movie, *Forest Gump*, is true. Sometimes I get the caramel and I feel great. Sometimes, I get the jelly piece with the investigative thumbprint in the bottom. Those are the "not-so-good" days. Mostly, I get the nougat pieces which are not great, but definitely are not bad.

In the following pages you will see how I deal with the disease. I hope this helps people, but I realize that everyone is different. What works for me may not work for others, but I encourage my fellow "parkies" to do their best to find some way to be positive, and continue living life. I also encourage family and friends of people with PD to continue to see them, and talk to them even though it may be difficult to witness the effects this disease has on someone you love.

It means a lot to be treated as a normal human being, and not like a member of a circus side show. Sometimes I want help and sometimes I don't. I know that it is difficult for caregivers to know when to help and when not to help. For me, I prefer that my wife let me try first and if she sees me start to get frustrated, then ask if I need help. With some things, you just know it is time to just walk way, such as putting in contacts lenses. One benefit from PD is that if you have any vanity left in your body, you lose it quickly. I didn't care if I had to wear the thickest black glasses in the world with a big piece of white tape on the nosepiece. There was no way I was going to endure the torture of trying to put contacts in on a daily basis. They would fall off my finger onto the floor, or I would poke myself in the eye, or it would stick on my nose or somewhere nearby. Since I had the DBS, I have been able to wear contacts again.

If you can laugh at yourself and if you can develop your faith, it can only help you. Search for reasons to be motivated.

Find people who inspire you. Think about why these people inspire you, and use those thoughts to help you through tough times. If you have fallen away from your faith, try to regain it. Think about why this happened and find your faith again. No matter what religion you practice, it will be there for you, if you look for it.

LIFE BEFORE DIAGNOSIS

I was born on February 14, 1966 in Northeast Philadelphia. My parents got divorced when I was three years old. My mother maintained custody of my sister, Patty, my brother, Jack, and me, but she received little else from a judge who must have been a complete idiot! My father kept the house, and only had to pay forty dollars a month in child support. Luckily, we were able to move in with my grandmother. My father should have stepped up, given my mother the house and paid more than forty dollars each month to support his kids. To her credit, my mother never told her kids about this or anything else regarding the divorce. I learned it long after my father died. My siblings and I grew up loving our dad, who was a lot of fun to be around. My mom could have easily bad-mouthed him, but never did. She is the nicest person I know by far. Learning about the whole situation surrounding the divorce and child support made a deep impression on me. I was determined to be successful as a husband and father.

One thing I preach to my two boys is to find the positive in a situation. Sometimes it is hard to find, sometimes it doesn't show for a while, and sometimes it does not outweigh the negative, but it is always there. Moving in with my grandmother gave her a reason to keep living. It was a huge positive that resulted from a very negative situation. She lived to be ninety-three years old, was a second mother to us, taught us so many lessons in life, and still lives inside each member of my family. I do not have one memory of her in a bad mood. I think of her when I have a bad day, and I feed off the positive attitude that she had to snap myself out of it. My grandmother's house was a three bedroom twin with one bathroom. My mom wanted to impact my grandmother as little as possible, so my mom, Patty, Jack, and I slept in the third bedroom. My mom and sister had about seventy-five percent of the third bedroom, and my brother and I had about twenty-five percent of the bedroom space. The two sections of the room were divided by an archway. My grandmother had her own room and my Uncle Jimmy, who had cerebral palsy, had his own room as well.

I was raised in St. Matt's parish in the Mayfair section of Philadelphia. One thing about Philly that I have found to be unique is if you are Catholic, and someone asks you where you are from in Philly, your first response is the parish where you were raised. The neighborhood name is not needed. To us, the parish name told us all we needed to know. If people actually told you their street address, it was easily translated to their parish, so, it worked both ways.

After my eight years at St. Matt's, I spent my next four years at Father Judge High School. I graduated in 1984 and was a member of the National Honor Society. From there, I spent four years at The Catholic

University of America. I was teasing my wife the other day, because she went to NYU and she has a nephew who is currently a sophomore at Harvard. She was telling me that her nephew, Kevin, is required to take four classes per semester. When Annie said that NYU is the same, I responded that my school apparently was much harder than Harvard or NYU, because we were required to take five classes per semester. We also had to take and pass a comprehensive test for our major at the end of our senior year in order to graduate. I earned a B.S. in mathematics, despite going through at least five math classes without understanding a word the teacher said. I'm not talking about them teaching over my head. I literally could not understand a word that came out of their mouths due to their thick accents. After graduation, I moved back to Philly and began looking for a job.

I began working with a company called Electronic Data Systems (EDS) in 1989. I met my wife two weeks after I started. She came into the office on her first day in a blue dress, and I knew that she was a catch if I could get her, and if I could decipher her accent. She was raised in Brooklyn, and still has the accent to prove it. We started out as friends working at an AT&T location. Sometimes her accent worked against her. I remember being in a class with her regarding *intralata* and *interlata* calls. Latas were just areas of the map defined by making a grid over a map. Each square represented a separate lata. The calls people made were billed based on whether the call was within a lata or from one lata to another. On the first day of class, the instructor begins talking about latas, and Annie turns to me and said, "What the heck does a ladder have to do with a phone call?" To her, *lata* and *ladder* were pronounced the same way. We began dating about a year later and got engaged two years later. We have been married since October16, 1993, over seventeen years. The other day, a friend of mine asked me if I ever saw the movie, *My Cousin Vinnie* with Joe Pesci and Marisa Tomei. I said, "Are you kidding me? Not only did I see it, that movie is my life!!" Just change the title to *My Wife Annie,* change the setting and rework the story a little. As far as the Brooklyn accent goes – dead on!

Annie is from a family of fourteen children, seven boys and seven girls. One of the things that attracted me to Annie was the importance of family that was instilled in her by her parents. If you truly need help and her family knows about it, they will be there for you, no matter what the status of your relationship is. When we first started dating, one weekend, we went to her brother, Pat's house to paint, and another weekend we put a new roof on her brother Chris' house. My friends started teasing me about it. "What are you doing next week, Kev, installing a new kitchen, painting again, building pyramids, recreating Stonehenge? Is there anything that Annie's family does not know how to do?" Each person in her family is expected to work hard and to do the job right, as are the in-laws when they help.

I never imagined that I would get PD at the age of twenty-six, but I did. I have to admit that the diagnosis hit me pretty hard because I had seen one of my uncles, Jim Nolan, slowly deteriorate due to this disease. Uncle Jim was a great guy by all accounts and had a great sense of humor. He was married to my dad's sister, Catherine. Before he passed away, he was in a wheelchair and was extremely difficult to understand.

Uncle Jim was able to handle his situation well, and he still threw out his barbs, which was essential on my dad's side of the family. You would get mauled if you couldn't fire back. If you couldn't take the heat, they turned the heat up on you.

There are a lot of people I have drawn on in dealing with this disease: my mom and her faith, my dad giving me a thick skin, my mom's brother, Jimmy Casey, who had cerebral palsy, the way my grand-mother always stayed upbeat despite being orphaned and separated from her siblings, Uncle Jim Nolan who battled PD, and my Uncle Jerry who has been a second father to me since my father died of cancer. I draw on the positive aspects of each person, and it helps me in my daily life and the decisions I make.

My wife and children are the center of my life and are my main motivation. The expectations I have for my kids, must be acted out by me or they will fall on deaf ears. I can't feel sorry for myself, because I don't want them to feel sorry for themselves. Two of my common reminders to my boys are to treat others the way you want to be treated and to ALWAYS do your best.

DIAGNOSIS

Just before turning twenty-seven, I got engaged to Annie. One day she asked me why my left thumb was shaking. I was about to say that it wasn't shaking, but when I looked down, it was shaking. I figured that it was a pinched nerve or something minor.

I went to a hand specialist, who then sent me to a neurologist. When the first neurologist said that I had PD, I left thinking that he was insane. To me, PD was something only old people got. Well, after three specialists all agreed on the diagnosis, I stopped labeling them as insane. Realizing that they know much more than I do, I figured they had to be right. So, sometimes I tease my wife that I was perfectly healthy prior to getting engaged. Honestly, I wouldn't change a thing. I would rather be married to her and have PD than not have her by my side. She has been the perfect wife.

My thoughts moved from denial to acceptance. I began to concentrate on two things, educating myself on PD, especially early onset, and on trying to set the right example on how to deal with having an illness like PD. My wife and I wanted children, so I knew that I couldn't feel sorry for myself. Every family has something, and I think that every parent would rather be the one suffering than watching a child suffer. It would eat me alive to watch my wife or children suffer. I would take on anything, if it meant that my children would be healthy. I figured that it also provided me with the opportunity to show how to remain positive and how to deal with adversity.

Annie and I have been married for over seventeen years and we have two boys, Conor, sixteen, and Ryan, fifteen. The boys being active in sports, has helped me to remain active. They both almost always beat me in any sports competition now that they have grown, but I still enjoy spending time with them. I definitely have lost some coordination and athletic ability, but exercise plays a huge factor in maintaining health and mobility. I have worked with a personal trainer for the past twelve years. She motivates me to come in for my workouts, which is important because I never know how I will feel. She always calls if I am not on time for my scheduled work out. Some days I just don't feel like going, but then she will call and thanks to her, I end up going in for my workout. About ninety percent of the times she calls, I end up working out. If you can afford a trainer, then I recommend getting one, because it gives you that little nudge that you sometimes need to get to the gym.

The medication sometimes makes me extremely tired. Plus, PD has made it harder for me to sleep at night. If I get three hours of straight sleep, that is a good night. On the bad nights I usually go down in my recliner so I don't disturb my wife. With PD, being tired is always a possibility, because the tired feeling hits out of nowhere sometimes.

LIFE AFTER DIAGNOSIS

What I lost and what I gained

I have to admit that I lost a lot of what I was, as a result of getting PD. The disease has had a negative impact on me physically, but probably the biggest impact has been my speech and cognitive function. Physically, I have improved after the DBS surgery in July of 2008. I still have stiffness and lost some coordination, but the shaking and dyskinesia are practically non-existent. The dystonia which causes my toes to curl under my feet, very rarely happens now. I still struggle with my speech, although that has improved a little since the operation also. Mentally, I struggle with holding a conversation with people due to the low volume of my voice, my increasing forgetfulness, and trouble focusing. I struggle with basic mathematical addition and subtraction, despite earning a degree in mathematics.

The cognitive impacts of the disease were the main reasons I had to stop working. I was falling asleep at my desk, and in meetings, and I could not stop it. There were times where I was writing code for enhancements to a Web based provisioning system, and I would fall asleep at my desk and wake up with three pages of the letter 'x' or whatever key my finger rested on. One particular time, I was asked to lead a group of five co-workers to fix a data problem we had. We had designed and evaluated possible solutions and ended up choosing one that I created. The next day we met again, but I had already forgotten the solution and the fact that I came up with the idea. That is when I started to think about going on disability.

I keep plugging away to make myself heard. Losing the ability to communicate would be a major blow, but I hope that I never reach that point. If it happens, I believe that I will find a way to overcome it or at least deal with it. It would take many potent, negative blows to beat me, because I don't give up easily. Part of the credit for this trait goes to the faith my mother instilled in me as far back as I can remember. Part of the credit goes to some of the inspirational people in my life, and part of it, goes to growing up in Philadelphia. It is a hard-working, blue collar city. You won't find many quitters in Philly, they get eaten alive at an early age. If you are hurt, you don't show it. You pick yourself up and keep on going. Nicknames last forever, so you don't want to give people any reason to give you a negative one.

I love Philly, and I think it gets a bad rap, as do its sports fans. Philly was a great place to grow up. If you hustle, play hard, and play to win, I guarantee that you'll be successful and loved there. This is the town that embraces players like Lenny Dykstra, Pete Rose, and Bobby Clarke. These are athletes that put their heart and soul into their games and got every ounce of ability out of their bodies. Play to your full capabilities, and they don't care if you fail. Put mock effort out there, and they'll smell it out and stomp you for it. If you've got the right stuff, you learn to appreciate that kind of a city. Philly is a town that either you get it – and you love it for its crustiness, or you don't get it and you hate it. Either way Philadelphians don't particularly care. It's that kind of blue-collar, hard-edged spirit that outsiders don't usually understand, but it contributes to a spirit of perseverance.

Philly helped to make me who I am today. The old phrase, "that which doesn't kill you, makes you stronger" never had a truer application. Philadelphians are hardworking and resilient. My sister is an example of this, despite being a ballerina and loving dancing and singing. Growing up where we did gave her toughness and a competitive edge that she still embraces. She is about as feminine as a girl can get, but I wouldn't want to compete against her in anything non-athletic. I think I can run backwards faster than she can run forwards, but, my Lord, she is smart as a whip and probably the most competitive person I know. You would not believe it when you first meet her, but if you challenge her to an intellectual game or even a card game, get ready to be trounced.

My recommendation to anyone battling a difficult situation, is to focus on the positives. Before I had to go on disability, I worked many hours, and did not get to spend much time with my kids. After going on disability, I didn't know what I was going to do with my time, but the best times I've had have been with my kids. If I had never gotten PD, I would never have been able to spend so much time with them.

PD has certainly robbed me of many things, but it has given me far more. It has given me more time with my family. It has helped me identify what is truly important in life. It has helped me to appreciate life and to realize that nothing is set in stone. I was cruising along with a good career, a fiancé who was beautiful, both physically and as a person. Then PD jumped in the way and guess what, my life is even better. Thanks to my family, my friends, and thanks to Philly! I feel like I will never give up, because if I do, these people and what this city represents will push me forward.

Wrong Medication

One day, several years ago, my pharmacist gave me the wrong medication. I received an anti-psychotic drug called Stelazine rather than Artane, a drug I took three times daily to relieve PD symptoms. The anti-psychotic drug was known to exacerbate PD symptoms. It was probably the scariest time in my life, because I was completely incapacitated.

During that time, my stride changed to a tiny shuffling of the feet. Each foot would creep along, literally at about two inches per stride. I couldn't sleep even though I was exhausted. I couldn't speak. At the same time, I had what felt like Restless Leg Syndrome (RLS). So I couldn't sit still, yet I could barely move. It was absolute torture. Now, when I think about it, I hope that wasn't a glimpse into my future. I thought my life was over with my kids and wife. The kids were very young at the time. I remember my older son asking me to have a catch with him. Normally, I jumped at any chance to play with my kids. Now I had to tell him that I couldn't play. He asked why and I told him that I was too sick. There I was, thirty-four years old, and I wasn't able to have a catch with my son.

It hit me that this could be my life over the next forty or fifty years. I love my wife and kids more than anything in the world and living like that would be extremely challenging. Both drugs happened to be next to each other on the shelf. The pharmacist that filled my prescription grabbed the wrong container. Both pills were almost identical in size, color and shape. Thank God I was able to overcome this bump in the road. There are times when I think the Stelazine did some permanent damage, but it would be difficult to prove.

Operation

The decision on whether or not I should go through with the DBS was one of the two most important, and challenging choices I have made. The other decision was asking my wife to marry me. As of now, I consider my record to be two wins and zero losses.

When you think about it, how many decisions make that big a difference in your life? You get a new car, a new house, even a new job. But choosing who to marry, you have to think way down the road. A car lasts several years. New jobs and houses often change several times in a lifetime. Choosing who you will marry should be thought of as a once in a lifetime decision. The choice to have brain surgery ranks up there, close to marriage.

Obviously, each brain surgery is a very delicate procedure. It doesn't matter how young and/or healthy the patient is. Prior to the DBS procedure, I did not want my kids to be worried, so I tried to be

41

nonchalant about it. In reality, I was confident about the procedure, but I knew there was a small possibility that I would not make it through the operations. My father passed away when I was fifteen, just after completing my freshman year at Father Judge High School. It was a time in a young man's life that he is just learning what it takes to become a man, and needs a father's love, advice, and also an occasional kick in the butt. So I wrote a long letter to them, covering as many areas as I could remember. It covered how to treat people, church, faith, religion, working with people, dealing with bad bosses, working hard, treating people with respect, meeting girls, and treating women with respect. My mother said to me before every date, "Treat her like you want your sister treated." Everything worked out with the operation and my wife didn't have to give the boys the letter.

Thank God, I found a great surgeon, Dr. Gordon Baltuch in Philadelphia at Pennsylvania Hospital. Dr. Baltuch and

Dr. Jurg Jaggi handled the operation and the immediate follow up. Dr. Matthew Stern is my neurologist that determines my medication levels and examines me every six months. I could not be happier with the level of care I received and continue to receive. I would highly recommend the "Parkinson's Disease and Movement Disorders Center" in Philadelphia.

The DBS procedure had three parts. For the first part, I was put under with general anesthesia. They secured some sort of halo type of device that helped them to figure out where the wires should go when it was time to insert them into my brain. I began to awake just as I was being pushed across the threshold of the operating room for part two of the procedure. The first words I heard were something to the effect of, "Hey wait …this isn't right." Now here I was, just coming out from under the anesthesia, and the first thing I heard was that something wasn't right! It was not exactly a ringing endorsement. It reminded me of my brother's hernia operation when he was in college. He was awake for the procedure and near the end, one of the surgeons said, "Did someone give this kid aspirin? I can't stop the bleeding." I'll take the "this isn't right comment" over the "bleeding" comment. I just put my faith in Dr. Baltuch and moved on. The next "pleasant" step was to have two holes drilled in my skull so they could gain access to my brain and insert the wires in the correct place. The wires have to be in the best possible location in order to have the best results. As they say in real estate, "Location, location, location." The first thing I saw once I was in the room was a DeWalt drill. That is the first time I gave it any thought that they use the same drill to go through my skull as the construction guys use to drill holes in wood studs etc. I don't know what kind of bit they used on my head, but I am pretty sure there aren't any special "bone boring bits" sold at your local Home Depot! By the way, don't try this at home! It's not exactly a do-it-yourself project!

Dr. Baltuch drilled the first hole and was finished in seconds flat. He then passed the DeWalt drill over to another doctor, who ended up struggling with drilling the hole. (My wife does tell me that I am hard-headed!) It started out ok, but then I think the progress hit a standstill. So then he started increasing the drill speed and pressing harder. Then, I began praying, and thinking "This guy is going to drill into my brain. If he does, I'll kill him!" Dr. Baltuch took over and was again done in seconds flat.

The next step was to identify where to place the wires by asking me to perform certain tasks such as, moving various parts of my body. The doctors asked me to sing a song. Well, I drew a complete blank. I thought of a decent number of song names, but not the words, until finally I remembered "Take Me Out to the Ballgame." It wasn't my best performance, but I belted it out anyway. Eventually, the DBS team found the correct place for the wires. Unfortunately, my singing voice didn't get any better. It's like the old joke where the man says, "Hey Doc, will I be able to play the piano after the operation?" The doctor says , "Sure." The man responds, "Great, because I can't play now!" The final stage consisted of inserting a pacemaker-like device that had wire connections to the brain. This device sits just below my right clavicle. From there, I went to the recovery room.

I later found out that at about the time that all of this was going on, my family (wife, mother, sister, brother, sister-in-law, two brothers-in law) and two friends were enjoying lunch at a nice restaurant in Philly. Here I was, wide awake, with a DeWalt drill, operating at what seemed to be like a zillion RPMs, boring two holes in my head. They, on the other hand, were relaxing, and enjoying a nice lunch. Actually, I don't blame them. Nobody wants to be stuck in a hospital waiting room all day.

What was even more amazing than the operation, was the response from my neighbors, friends, even people that I didn't know in the community. Prayer groups were praying for me, and I didn't even know it until almost a year had passed. Some friends organized meals to be made for us. Others donated money or gift cards to help my family get through the recovery. I can't tell you how touching it was or how much I appreciate the prayers, gifts and visits in the hospital and at home. It is times like this that you find out who your friends are. It is also times like this that renew your faith in mankind.

Recovery Room

My recovery from the operation went remarkably well. Overall, I was in the hospital for a little over two days. I went in very early on Monday, July 20th and went home on Wednesday, July 22nd. The surgeons were very happy with the results, and I was even happier.

When I came out from under the anesthesia, the first person that came in the recovery room was my wife, Annie. We looked at each other and she started crying. It took all I had to hold myself together and to assure her that I was fine. She took the picture of me that is now on the cover of this book about two hours after the DBS procedure was over. I wanted her to show the kids that I was alive and well, which is why I gave the "thumbs up" with both hands.

My brother came in later and was ready with a wise crack as usual. He had the line of the day, saying that I needed all these visitors like I needed another hole in the head, knowing of course about the two freshly drilled holes in my head from the DBS. Actually, I felt pretty good and was happy to have the visitors. Two days later, I checked out, thrilled to be heading home to continue my recovery.

INSPIRATIONAL
PEOPLE

Grandmother

My grandmother, Alice Regina Casey, was something special. She was a role model to me, and I think of her, and the way she lived her life practically every day. First of all, she was the nicest person you could ever meet. She loved people and she loved her family even more. She also was tough as nails, but very dignified. It is a rare combination, but she pulled it off. She wore a dress every day no matter what her plans were. She never raised her voice or hand on any of us. Yet, we knew when we did something wrong. She just calmly, but sternly corrected us.

Because my grandmother was so friendly and easy to talk to, people who grew up on our street would come back and visit her sometimes fifteen to twenty years later and say that they had to come see her while they were in town. It was not unusual for these former neighbors to stop by our house, totally unannounced. My grandmother loved every minute of it. She immediately went into hostess mode: "What can I get you to eat or drink?" She rolled through five to ten options for them to make a selection. Basically, she presented her visitors with choices until they said yes to something. If it turned out that she didn't have the selection in the house, she sent my brother or me out the back door to ride our bikes to the store so we could buy it and bring it back. Once we got back, she served it to her guests, as if it was no trouble at all. She wanted everyone to feel comfortable and welcome in her house. She was one of the happiest people I have ever known. My grandmother could not have had a more positive view on life, even though she had a rough life.

My grandmother was orphaned at about the age of ten. Both parents passed away within six months of each other. Her brothers and sisters were separated and sent to live with either relatives or family friends. They were able to stay in contact with each other, but it would be days or weeks between visits. Back then, people did not have phones in their houses. She was told that she was going to live with a police-man's family whose wife was confined to a wheelchair. So, she went from living with her parents and siblings, having fun with her friends, to helping this lady clean and dress herself, cooking all the meals, doing laundry, and cleaning the house.

My grandmother's closest friend was her sister, Great Aunt Anna. Despite being separated as children, they remained very close. In fact, they spoke to each other on the phone every day once they were married and had a phone in the house. As I grew up, my grandmother sat in the chair next to the phone, rocking back and forth, and laughing for at least an hour each day with Aunt Anna. As they reached old age and their hearing started to fail, they still spoke and laughed every day, though I honestly think that they only heard about ten percent of what each other said. They were just happy that they could hear each other's voice, even if they could not quite hear the words. The funny thing is that her bad hearing has helped me recognize when someone can't hear me, but doesn't want to ask me to repeat myself again. Generally, my grandmother would try to read the look on the person's face and go from there. If the person smiled, she would give a little laugh or chuckle. If the person looked serious, she would nod her head and say something like "Mm-hmm." So, she is still helping me get through life even today. When I see people fake a laugh, I know that they did not hear me.

I know everyone means well, so I just base my decision on whether or not I am going to repeat my comment, on how important it is to the discussion, or how funny the comment is. There is nothing worse than repeating a joke four or five times, thinking that they didn't hear you, when in reality, they just didn't think the joke was funny.

My grandmother was about five foot three and one hundred pounds, but she had the heart of a champ. I remember when she slipped and fell in the kitchen and broke her knee cap. Not one whimper came out of her mouth. She simply said to me, "Kev, just help me over to the chair and I'll be fine." She was eighty-five years old! She ended up having knee surgery and going through therapy, but she miraculously made a complete recovery.

About five years later, my grandmother fell and broke her hip. Again, she did not shed a tear. She didn't even want the ambulance to come take her to the hospital. She recovered from hip surgery, but unfortunately passed away about three years later. She has been and will continue to be with me every day of my life. Whether I picture her smiling face, or think of one of her many sayings, or just remember her overall positive attitude at all times, I think of her daily and I miss her company even more.

Mother's Prayer and Faith

Prayer and faith go hand in hand. If you have faith in God, you will pray, at least in times of need.

There are different ways to pray. My grandmother prayed by having more of a conversation with God. She said that she could never seem to concentrate long enough to say an "Our Father," or a rosary. She would ask God to forgive her, or to help her, or someone else to get through a sickness, or to give her strength to do his will. She would ask for these things using the same phrasing that she would ask a friend for help. I always thought that this showed how dear to her heart she held her faith in God and the Blessed Mother, and I can't forget St. Anthony. St. Anthony was called upon whenever something was lost, and he never failed her. She would search the house while saying, "Come on Anthony! I need your help finding..." She still prayed, just not in the traditional sense. Then there is my mother. She has no problem saying prayers. She says rosaries, novenas etc. on a daily basis. For both of them, God is a rock to lean on in bad times and a rock to thank for His help in good times.

There are many people who do a great deal of praying in their lives, but I don't think anyone prays as much as my mother. There are sequestered nuns and monks that do nothing but pray, and I think she still manages to pray more.

She sends intentions to sequestered orders to pray for the things she wants. When I say things, I mean not materialistic things, but things such as world peace, patience, or to help an ailing friend. Most of her prayers, I would wager, are for her children and grandchildren. She has those sequestered priests and nuns basically working for her around the clock with all of her petitions. Some day, I swear she is going to start getting billed for the time. She is like the CEO of prayer, who delegates to her co-workers.

To say the least, my mother has done a lot of praying for me over my lifetime. As Bill Murray said in the movie "*Caddyshack,*" "So I've got that going for me, which is nice." I have done a lot of praying as well. Two things stand out in my head that I can picture my mother saying. One is, "There are no atheists in a foxhole." This means that when faced with a life and death situation, you would be surprised how important God becomes. The second is "Sometimes faith is all you have left." She means that there will be times in most of our lives that all will seem lost. You won't know where to go or what to do. Maybe, you know you are going the wrong way, but you don't know how to fix it. In those moments, she would say to me, "Your faith will carry you through. " I thank her, because it has definitely gotten me through some tough times. Her unwavering faith is the greatest gift she ever gave me.

One last saying from my mother that has had a major influence on me is "Can't means won't." You can do anything. It is a matter of whether or not you want to do it. If you truly want something you have to work hard to get it.

Uncle Jimmy

My Uncle Jimmy was born with cerebral palsy and could not even walk until he was four years old. My grandmother had to carry him on her hip for those four years. She took him to see many specialists, but no one could help him. People told her that she would damage her hip carrying a four-year-old around, but she did what she had to do and continued to carry him. He probably weighed about forty pounds, almost half her weight, but she handled it and glared at anyone who gave him funny looks.

My grandmother instilled the importance of family, and loyalty in her children, who in turn, instilled it in me, my siblings and cousins. She passed on mottos such as, "family first", and "brothers before others." So, my mother and her siblings made sure their brother was treated nicely by others.

My uncle finally began walking at age four, and my grandmother's hip had no problems until she broke it when she was ninety. As far as my uncle goes, he never stopped walking. The man had his faults, but he was as dedicated to his job as anyone I have ever known. Uncle Jimmy was thrilled just to have a job. He did not use one sick day for twenty-five years at his job at a Cerebral Palsy Center. He was the first one there in the morning, at about 5:30 am, to open the building, and clean the floors.

Not even the 1983 Southeastern Pennsylvania Transportation (SEPTA) strike stopped him from getting to work. He walked just about ten miles each way to work; in other words, he was hoofing it twenty miles each day. Well, the strike lasted one hundred and eight days, and he did not miss a single day. Due to his cerebral palsey, he had an awkward gait and heavy feet. His body took a pounding. He wore through shoes in less than a month. At a clip of one hundred miles per week, Uncle Jimmy was going through shoes faster than Secretariat. I'll borrow another line from "Forrest Gump" where the narrator said "He couldn't walk until he was four but once he did walk, he did it more and better than most!"

His perseverance is something I store in the back of my mind, and it has motivated me to keep plugging away when I was at work and also in my dealings with PD. I was able to go over ten years at work without using a sick day, before the PD symptoms made it too difficult to continue working.

My uncle's trials and tribulations with cerebral palsy have helped motivate me to keep on fighting. I remember someone gave him a t-shirt that simply said, "No problem." That was perfect for him. He didn't let his condition stop him. If you asked him to do something for you his answer was "No problem!" I try to follow in his footsteps by not complaining and not letting PD stop me.

Sandy Fritsch

Sandy is a fellow "parkie" and friend. She, among other things, runs support groups out of the "Parkinson's Disease and Movement Disorders Center" in Philadelphia. When I was diagnosed with PD, I really did not want to go to support groups. My symptoms were relatively mild, so seeing people in worse shape than me, felt like a depressing glimpse into my future. At the time, I was not really ready for that. I figured that it would make it harder to stay positive if I went to these meetings. Plus, being twenty-seven years old, I felt that I was out of place, but Sandy changed all of that. Most of the people at her meetings had early onset PD, which is basically defined as being diagnosed younger than fifty years old.

Eventually, I decided to try one of Sandy's meetings. She sounded like she had a positive attitude. I never was a big talker. Part of the reason for that is that my mother, sister and brother talk quite a bit, as did my grandmother. Being the youngest, I found it hard to be heard. So, I became a good listener that just threw wise cracks out at whoever was there. I figured that I had to make what I say count. So, if I can come up with something funny, it pretty much pops out. When I got to the meeting, I couldn't stop talking. I left that meeting thinking that the people must have thought to themselves, "Will somebody shut this guy up?" I found that I had a lot more to say than I thought I would. I went into the meeting thinking, "How are these people going to help me?" I left the meeting thinking, "Hopefully, some of what I said helped someone there." I enjoyed this meeting more than I could have ever expected, because it reminded me of that Christmas motto, "It is better to give than receive."

I thank Sandy for that. She maintains a upbeat meeting and promotes positive thoughts. She has made a positive influence on so many lives of both people with PD and people without it. The fact that she does this while dealing with PD is amazing.

My Dad and Uncle Jerry

As I mentioned before, my father really loved to get his digs in and tease the people close to him. I have to admit that he definitely rubbed off on me in this area. Just ask my wife, children, and my close friends. By being this way, I think he was trying to do two things. First of all, he got a good laugh himself and usually everybody else did as well. I also think my dad wanted to give his kids a thick skin to prepare us for the outside world.

When I was a little kid, I was pretty sensitive to my dad's comments. Part of the reason probably was due to my parents divorce when I was three years old. I don't know how long it took for it to sink in that he was just kidding, but it eventually did. Unfortunately, he died of cancer when I was fifteen, so I never really had a chance to get to know him as well as I would have liked, but I do have memories of vacations, watching sports, and playing sports with him. Another thing about my father is that he had to be in a great deal of pain, but he never showed it in front of his children. I know I don't remember it. I do remember him losing a ton of weight as the cancer took control and that he was so weak that he couldn't move his legs even when he was in bed. Like my grandmother, he set an example on how to deal with illness. I try to follow their example in my dealings with PD.

After he died, I really struggled for a while. I had just finished my freshman year in high school. Sophomore year was probably the toughest year of my life. There were times that I would think of him and it would be hard to hold it together, knowing that he was dead. There were also times when I could have used his advice, and felt that I had no one to go to for help. There are certain things for which you can't go to your mother, no matter how great she is. If your dad isn't around, you have to figure out some things on your own. It may be dealing with girls, although I don't think any man has completely figured that one out yet anyway! It may be dealing with a bully in school. It could be something as simple as dealing with a slump in baseball.

At that time, I began to look at my Uncle Jerry as a father figure. He and I had a great relationship even when I was a little kid. I was the skinniest kid you could imagine, even though I ate an unbelievable amount of food. I think this is where my uncle and I first connected. He had a way of making you feel special in some way. My way involved a bowl or four of spaghetti and meatballs. He used to get a kick out of the fact that I could eat so much. I have to admit that there were times that I kept eating just to get a reaction out of him. He loved to eat as well and would laugh that I was the only person still eating. I didn't go to him for advice so much as I observed how he acted, and how he loved his wife and children. He loves his family full throttle, and would run through a brick wall to help them. He also isn't afraid to tell his wife and kids that he loves them. My uncle is no push-over. He grew up in Kensington, which is and was a very tough section in Philly. He was also a great athlete and played football and baseball at West Catholic High School. More importantly, Uncle Jerry was also a great student. I decided to look to his example when I was faced with challenges from that point forward in my life. I wasn't a good enough athlete to make my high school sports teams. My best sports were baseball and street hockey. I broke my arm playing tackle football in the street (not my brightest decision) just before baseball tryouts my freshman year. I never bothered with baseball after that. I graduated high school at about five-foot eight inches, weighing in at a staggering one hundred and twenty-five pounds. With that kind of physique, football was out too. My high school had close to 1,500 boys in it, so you had to be an exceptional athlete to play on any of its sports teams. So, I concentrated on my grades, and earned a couple partial scholarships and grants to The Catholic University of America in Washington D.C.

The main lessons I learned from Uncle Jerry are to love your family wholly and selflessly, and that there is nothing wrong with telling your wife and children that you love them. If you never say it, they may never know it.

YOU HAVE TO LAUGH

I truly believe that laughter is the best medicine. You have to be able to laugh at yourself, especially if you are going to laugh at others(in a nice way). I certainly do not condone teasing to the point of being downright mean. My dad was very funny, usually at someone's expense, but never mean-spirited. He knew who he could tease and who was too sensitive. If he knew you could handle it, he was relentless.

I have to say that my brother, who is about one year older than I am, plays a close second to my dad in this department. He laughs more easily than me, and has a very contagious laugh, so he gets everyone else going. The teasing was all good natured though. At least, most of it was. So, pretty much my entire family laughs very easily. We are a comedian's dream crowd. One day in college, I was called up on stage to try not to laugh as three comedians performed their routines. If I made it past all three without laughing, I would have received a prize of some sort. Well, I lasted all of fifteen seconds before they sent me back to the crowd.

The way I look at life is this – you don't know how long you have, so you might as well enjoy it. Money can't buy happiness. You have to be yourself. Happiness comes from within. If you find laughter on a fairly regular basis, you will be happier.

Find what makes you laugh. If it is a comedian you like then watch a couple of his routines. It could be a comedy show or movie. Just find something happy and funny. It will help free you from the daily woes and worries of dealing with PD. You could try passing some jokes on to a friend. The only thing better than laughing is making others laugh and laughing with them.

In one of his books, Michael J. Fox said that he tells his kids every day, "Choose to have a great day." I think this is awesome! I immediately started saying that to my two boys, Conor and Ryan. Of course, they immediately started rolling their eyes. It really is the truth. It is up to you to make your day a good one. Bad things are going to happen to everyone. You can either let those things ruin your day, or you can move on with a positive attitude, and finish your day in a proud, positive and productive manner. And let's face it, no one wants to be around someone who complains all the time.

I know that some people suffer from depression, which is a tough condition. My heart goes out to those people, because there is only so much a person can do when under the cloud of depression. Watching a comedian is not going to cut it. I don't mean to be simplistic, especially regarding depression. I am certainly no expert. However, for those who do not suffer with depression, if you can continue to laugh and/or make others laugh, you will be happier and healthier.

I was at a symposium on aging once in Westchester, New York, and the speaker had recently published a book on people who lived past one hundred years. The one common thread among them is that they laughed every day, often and easily.

DUI Checkpoint

I went to a playoff game (Philadelphia Flyers vs. New York Rangers) with my brother Jack, back in 1997. We had a couple beers during the game and a couple after while we waited for the parking lot to thin out.

When the lot cleared, I headed up Highway I-95 North to my exit in Bucks County, PA. I was less than a mile from my house when I came around a bend in the road and saw signs saying "DUI Checkpoint Ahead." I thought that I should be ok, but you never know.

When the police officers saw me shaking so much, they probably thought that I was nervous and that they had a drunk driver dead to rights. I got the usual question, "Why are you so nervous?" I responded with the usual answer, "I have Parkinson's." That has gotten me out of four tickets over the past twenty years. I say that only as a statement of fact, not to brag about avoiding a ticket. It has been about ten years since I was pulled over, so I have slowed down over the past several years. I think that the police officers who let me go just felt bad for me. I certainly don't recommend trying to avoid getting a ticket this way. Anyway, I followed the police officer to the back of the car to begin the sobriety tests. I said the alphabet frontwards and backwards. I walked a straight line and followed his fingers with my eyes without moving my head.

Finally, a late-arriving officer says, "Your speech seems a little slurred. Are you sure you did not drink too much?" I said, "Well officer, I have Parkinson's, and it affects my speech." He responded very quickly, as to show he wasn't buying it. He was just doing his job and he immediately responded with a slight "I gotcha" grin, saying "Does Parkinson's affect a breathalyzer?" I laughed a little, but made sure not to be disrespectful and said, "I can't say that it does." As it turned out, I passed the breathalyzer test, and drove home.

Patty's Wedding

My sister Patty got married on July 20, 2007. It was one of the worst tremor days that I ever had. I don't know why, it just seems like some days are worse than others. I have identified certain things that aggravate my tremors, such as too much caffeine, too much sugar, mental and physical stress. I swear there are times that nothing helps slow the tremor. An elephant could sit on my left hand and somehow that tremor would keep on going in a way that only the Energizer bunny could rival.

My sister was dressed in her wedding gown, waiting inside the Ritz Carlton Hotel in Philadelphia. I was outside in my tuxedo, standing on the sidewalk waiting for her to come out, so we could get in the limousine and head over to the church. As I said, I was having a bad day with the tremors, noticeably shaking to all who passed by. Instead of the strange looks I was getting from other people, this one man looked inside and saw my sister in her wedding gown, then turned to me and said, "Man you must be the groom, you're shaking like a leaf. Don't worry, you'll be alright. You'll be alright." How could I not laugh at that? This is a case where I could either laugh at myself or let an innocent comment ruin my day. This still brings a smile to my face when I think of it.

Stand Still

When I was a kid growing up in Philadelphia, I played quite a bit of street hockey. Back in the 1970s and 1980s this was a huge sport in Philly with the popularity of the Philadelphia Flyers, also known as the "Broad Street Bullies."

When I was about thirty years old my friends and I decided to join a street hockey league. One night on my way to a game, I noticed a store on the left side of the road, and thought I would stop in for a Gatorade for my game. There were three different driveways, and I realized that I was going towards the wrong one. The correct driveway entrance was about fifteen yards up the road on the left. The problem was that I was on the wrong side of the road. So, I thought to myself, I hope no policemen are watching this as I gunned it on the wrong side of the solid yellow line, and sped into the parking lot of the 7-Eleven.

I was still thinking to myself that I hoped no police cars were nearby as I opened the car door and started to get out of the car. To my surprise, as soon as I stood up, I heard, "Stand still!" over what seemed to be a megaphone. Well, the first thought was, "You've got to be kidding me. You are yelling at me to stand still when all I did was commit a traffic violation." My second thought was, "Hey I have Parkinson's. It is pretty much impossible to stand still!"

The next thing I hear is, "Stan Still, please report to the front desk." I couldn't believe it. As it turned out, there was a car dealership across the street paging a salesman named Stan Still. The timing was unbelievable! I had a huge sigh of relief, laughed and walked into the 7-Eleven.

I found out later that there was a car salesman by the name of Stan Stilowatski, or something like that, working at that dealership across the street from 7-Eleven.

Apparently, they shortened his name and called him "Still" or "Stan Still" to make it easier. Easier for them, maybe, but not for me! I almost had a nice, easy heart attack!

Public Bathrooms

When you have PD, dealing with embarrassment in public, or strange looks from people is part of the daily experience. Well for men, going into a public bathroom is up there on the list. Just think about what people are thinking when they see your hands, or body shaking vigorously as you are hunched over the urinal.

More than once, I heard comments as I played the role of the shaking guy who is taking forever to relieve himself. The comments range from a simple "What is taking so long!" to "I don't have to go any more" to "More than three shakes means you're enjoying it!"

Now you might say, just go in a stall. Well that was an option until Senator Larry Craig from Idaho was involved in that incident in a bathroom at the Minneapolis-St. Paul airport. He was accused of soliciting sex from the person in the next stall by tapping his foot. Tapping your foot is apparently a signal to the guy in the stall next to you that you are interested in gay sex. Well, I'd take public ridicule and use the urinal rather than the alternative, because my left foot tapped pretty darn fast at times and the last thing I needed was sex of any kind in a public bathroom.

I don't know how these signals get started, but I wish they would stop. I haven't used a stall since I found this out. I guess the Parkinson community has left a lot of these people feeling like they were teased by our tapping feet then walking out. I wonder what happens when you tap both feet. Actually, I don't think I want to know!

I don't think that Senator Craig was ever convicted. Regardless of the outcome, it was the first time I heard of that signaling system. This is something that should probably be in the pamphlets about PD for new patients!

Pre OP urine test

As anyone who has had an operation knows, you are required to go through pre-op testing. It ranges from height and weight, to blood pressure and providing a urine sample. Ah yes, the urine sample. It seems simple enough. However, when the whole left side of your body is shaking like a nudist in the North Pole, it is no longer simple. As it turned out, it was probably the hardest thing I had to do throughout the entire operation!

The nurse handed me a little cup and directed me towards the bathroom that I was supposed to use. Looking at the little cup, I said to myself, "This ought to be interesting." Well, I walked in the bathroom, closed the door and turned on the light. Then, the fun began! I looked down at the cup and tried to think how I could fill it without spilling or spraying urine all over the bathroom and myself.

I wedged my left arm and shoulder against the wall, lifted my left foot off the floor, and thanked God that it was a private bathroom so I did not have to worry about getting propositioned for tapping my foot. I put the cup in my left hand and held my left hand above the toilet. Then, with my right hand I directed the flow into the cup. All this while still wedged against the wall and standing on one foot. I don't think the Flying Wallendas, the famous tightrope walkers, could have pulled off this balancing act. Somehow I got it done and with my mission accomplished, I exited the bathroom, handed the cup to the nurse and said, "I'd be careful with this one, because I don't think I could repeat that feat!"

Voice therapist (late for appointment)

My voice problems and therefore the inability to communicate is probably the most frustrating thing that I deal with as a result of having PD. At one point, my neurologist recommended that I go to speech therapy. Well, it turned out that this was quite an ironic twist. My wife was born and raised in Brooklyn, NY. Let me tell you, it would take you about five seconds to figure that out if you spoke to her and heard that accent. To this day, I still tease her about it and we have known each other for twenty-one years. Before we had kids, I would always tease her and say that if our children spoke like her, they would have to attend speech therapy to rid themselves of that accent.

Well look what happened, I had to go to speech therapy! Sometimes life is not fair. Well maybe it is. Maybe it was just payback for all that teasing I did. As it turned out, my two boys do not have a Brooklyn accent and they did not require speech therapy. In actuality, I love her accent. I think part of the reason is the sound, and part is that the accent is a frequent source of material that I can use to give her a hard time. Luckily, Annie is a good sport, and believe me, her tongue is at least as sharp as mine.

Anyway, I signed up with the speech therapist, Joan Levicoff at the "Parkinson's Disease and Movement Disorders Center." Well, if Joan said once, she said a thousand times, "Kevin slow down and speak louder." One day I was running late for an appointment, so I called Joan to tell her that I was running late. Joan answered and we both said hello. The rest of the conversation went something like this:

Kevin: "Joan, I am running about fifteen minutes late for my appointment."

Joan: "Louder Kevin"

Kevin (a little louder): "I am running about fifteen"

Joan: "I can't hear you, Kevin!"

Kevin(definitely louder): "I am going to be about fifteen minutes late!"

Joan (noticeably louder): "Louder Kevin! I can't hear you!"

Now I was thinking that this is ridiculous. I was pretty much screaming into the phone and Jane could not hear me. I said to myself, "Is this my wife or my therapist?" I knew that we heard each other when we said hello. Then, something clicked and I realized that I accidentally hit the mute button on my cell phone! Well, at least we had a good laugh.

Even after the operation, my voice challenges the hearing of the people I know and meet, but it is better than it was. My wife disagrees. We do not argue often, but when we do, it is usually over my low voice and her bad hearing.

Since I am writing this book, I'll take advantage of that fact and say, the fight usually starts when Annie makes a complete guess at what I said. For instance, I said something to her once and she thought I said, "The monkey drove the car to Tokyo." My response was, "Now why would I say that. If you are going to guess, make it one that has some possibility of being true!" It lasts about ten minutes and we are back to normal. I couldn't ask for a better wife. She is truly a wonderful person.

Acting Out My Dreams

About six months after my DBS operation, I began to have a problem where I acted out my dreams while asleep. At first it was funny. The first time it happened, I heard Annie scream, "Ow!" in the middle of the night. I woke up just as she said that and asked her what happened. She said, "You hit me in the head!" I responded that I had a dream where I was knocking on the door. While acting out the dream, I must have knocked on the back of her head. I said that it was a good thing the people in my dream answered the door, or I would have knocked again! She didn't find that comment quite as funny as I did. As it turned out, she was fine. The problem continued though.

I went through most of the major sports. Annie saw my legs going very fast, as if I was running, and then my arm came flying out in front of me, as if I was throwing a pass. I fell asleep on the sofa and kicked the coffee table with my right foot while dreaming of playing soccer. I hit Annie with my left arm while dreaming of blocking someone's shot in basketball. Then I head-butted the night table next to our bed. I trapped Annie's leg in a scissor hold with my two legs because I had a dream where I was in a fight with two people who just robbed a store. Finally, I spoke to Dr. Stern, my neurologist, and he gave me a prescription to stop that from happening. So, now Annie doesn't have to sleep with one eye open. I teased her over the years that we have been married that I needed to sleep with one eye open, since she was from Brooklyn and she probably would seek revenge!

Broken hand and finger

A couple of years before my DBS surgery, I asked for a toaster oven as a gift. I just wanted to use it for cooking frozen pizza and food like that rather than heating up the large gas oven. Well, Annie came home with an enormous toaster oven one day and put it on the counter. She then said that it was too big to put on the counter so she wanted to store it in the closet and take it out only when we needed it. I suggested that we just buy a smaller one and return the toaster oven she bought, which I think could be used to cook a turkey on Thanksgiving! Although it was supposed to be my gift, somehow she was able to get her way and we kept the turkey toaster oven. I never use it because to me, it is inconvenient. The whole purpose in getting a toaster was for convenience!

In May, 2008, two months prior to my DBS, my older son broke and dislocated his wrist. He did a great job in staying calm. We went to the hospital and the orthopedic doctor, had to reset his wrist which is very painful. He handled it all very well. Not only didn't he curse, he barely made a sound in regards to the pain. He ended up casted for two months and is fine now.

About three weeks after the DBS procedure, I noticed that Annie had left the toaster oven out on the counter. I had just been told in a follow up visit after the DBS, that I had to be careful not to bang my head, because if I get a cut on my head, it could lead to infection, which could cause me to have the DBS implant removed. So, I noticed that the toaster oven was not plugged in, and I leaned my head over the back of it to find the plug.

When I stood back up, I banged my head on the corner of the oven vent and it was a direct hit exactly where one of the wires was inserted into my brain. In an instant, I thought that I just ruined everything, and that I was going to have to get the operation redone. I was furious, and I without thinking, punched the oven vent, which is unfortunately made out of metal. The next thing anyone heard was, "I think I busted my hand!" "Great move knuckle-head," I thought to myself. I was cursing in the kitchen until Ryan checked my head and everything was ok. So then Conor reminded me that he did not curse when he broke his wrist. Sometimes, I guess that we learn from those we are trying to teach.

About two days after I got the cast off, I was goofing around with my boys and I slid down the stairs in a sleeping bag. Just as I got near the bottom, one of my dogs jumps in front of me. Trying to avoid her, I turned to my side, but caught my finger on the end of one of the steps, and it snapped my finger out to the side. Home for a month, and I already had two breaks!

Are you nervous?

I can't tell you how many times people have stopped to help me to ask if I was ok or if I was nervous, or just stare at me like I had three heads.

Whenever I started a new position at work and dealt with new people, I always had to explain that I didn't shake because I was nervous. That was one thing that bothered me for awhile after being diagnosed. People staring at you is bad enough, but when you see them laughing to themselves, it is infuriating. You wonder what they are thinking. Whenever I gave a presentation at work, I started by explaining that I had PD. That way, the audience and I both seemed to get more focused. The audience actually retained information instead of looking at me thinking, "Who is this nervous guy up there delivering the presentation?"

One of my old friends at EDS was Rod David. He is African-American, and my wife and I were invited to his 35th birthday party. After being at the party for about a half hour, Rod's nine year old nephew came over to me to tell me not to be nervous or worry because no one was going to hurt me. I laughed and assured him that I wasn't worried and that I had Parkinson's disease and it made me shake. I was the only white guy there at the time so he must have thought that was why I was shaking. He was a very nice young man. I thought it took courage to come up to me and ask me that question to try to make me feel comfortable.

Smithwick's

My cousin Timmy more than once complimented me on never complaining about my condition. He lives about five minutes away from me, so he has invited me over to watch numerous Notre Dame games, Eagles games, etc. Before I had the DBS surgery, my left hand, arm and leg all shook pretty badly. Tim has a beer called Smithwick's, which is imported from Ireland, on tap all day, every day. He loves this beer and really should be a spokesperson for it. I have spoken to other people in my neighborhood and had more than one say that they know a guy that loves this Smithwick's beer so much that it is the only beer he drinks. When I ask if his name is Tim Mulhern, I always get the response, "Yeah, how did you know?", and I just say that he is my cousin.

Anyway, whenever I went over Timmy's house, he would always go down the basement to get me beer from the Smithwick's tap. If I stood up to get a refill, Timmy

would stand up and say, "I'll get it for you."
I thought nothing of it other than thinking
that his hospitality was extraordinary.

After the DBS surgery, which was so successful in stopping the tremors in my hands,
suddenly things were different. Now when
I go to Timmy's house to watch a game or
go to a party, I have to get my own beer.
When I started joking about it, he said that
he used to get it for me because he didn't
want me spilling all his precious Smithwick's
beer all over the rugs! I'm pretty sure that
Tim wasn't too concerned about the rugs.

Tim is a great guy and I appreciate all
he has done for me. I have to admit that
Smithwick's is my favorite beer too, so I
understand why he was so protective of his
supply.

CONCLUSION

So, in a nutshell, here is my philosophy on dealing with this disease and other challenges in life. Try to find a positive. There is always one there. It may not outweigh the negative, but it is there somewhere. Work on your faith, no matter what your religion is. Faith gives you hope when everything seems to be crumbling around you. As long as you have hope, you can find the strength to keep on going. If you happen to be an atheist, I can't help much in the faith department, other then to repeat what my mother says, "There are no atheists in a foxhole." My Uncle Jack, her brother, told her that shortly after returning home from the South Pacific as a marine in World War II fighting against the Japanese. Find inspirational stories or people that will motivate you to keep pushing forward. Compete against PD, as if it is a tangible entity that you can square off against. Do not let it get the best of you. Do not let it win! Finally, laugh as much as possible. Try your best to find humor in your life, or find it watching kids play, seeing how much they laugh each day. Bottom line, try to find laughter somewhere, because it is very therapeutic.

I hope you enjoyed the book as much as I enjoyed writing it. I hope this book helps some of my fellow parkies in dealing with PD. Also, I sometimes think that this disease and others are harder on the caregivers than they are on the patients. Hopefully, they get something out of it as well.

If I left anyone out, I apologize. Just because you didn't get mentioned in this book, doesn't mean that you are not important to me. There are many family members, and friends that have and will continue to play an important role in my life. I thank you all for your support and prayers.

Finally, I hope I can maintain a positive attitude as this disease progresses on me. If I don't and anyone that I know sees me feeling sorry for myself, please give me a "Thumbs Up" and tell me to be positive.

Made in the USA
Charleston, SC
21 December 2011